Love Your Books
by Angie Rowe

ILLUSTRATED BY
Natalia Rowe

DESIGNED BY
Dan Clarke - Telford Repro

"For all the people who dedicate their time helping animals to live a wonderful life" 🐾

Angela Rowe
angie.rowe@loveyour-books.com

www.loveyour-books.com

Love Your Rabbit

Content Copyright © Angela Rowe
                    Protect My Work 2018
Illustration Copyright © Natalia Rowe
                    Protect My Work 2018

ISBN 978-1-9163572-6-6

Love Your Books

by Angie Rowe

Love your Cat

Love your Hamster

Love your Dog

Love your Budgie

Love your Horse

Love your Fish

To Parents, Carers & Teachers

These 'Love Your' Books are to help bring out empathy, compassion and kindness within your child and their natural loving nature to shine through.

To love all animals domestic and wild, whether big or small is one of the best traits to have.

Cruelty should **NEVER** belong in a child's heart.

Your Rabbit needs food

Without food

Without water

Your Rabbit needs hay

I love hay! It makes me feel warm and cosy. I can nibble on it as well

Without hay

Your Rabbit needs a hutch

Without a hutch

Your Rabbit needs excercise and cuddles

Without excercise and cuddles

DON'T

- HIT YOUR RABBIT

- PULL YOUR RABBIT BY THEIR EARS

- HOLD THEM TOO HIGH IN CASE YOU DROP THEM

- LEAVE THEM IN A HUTCH ALL THE TIME

IT IS CRUEL

DO

- FEED YOUR RABBIT A VARIED DIET

- GIVE THEM PLENTY OF FRESH WATER

- GIVE THEM LOVE AND ATTENTION

- BRUSH YOUR RABBIT

- GIVE PLENTY OF EXCERCISE

LOVE YOUR
RABBIT
WITH ALL YOUR
HEART

REMEMBER
YOUR RABBIT LOVES YOU
VERY MUCH

In a world
where you can
be anything
BE KIND

Colour me
So ph CRAZY

Printed in Great Britain
by Amazon